D1240489

Are you a Centipede?

KINGFISHER
LONDON & NEW YORK

Copyright © Macmillan Publishers International Ltd 2019
Text copyright © Judy Allen 2019
Illustrated by Fiona Osbaldstone (Advocate Art Agency)

Published in the United States by Kingfisher,
175 Fifth Avenue, New York, NY 10010
Kingfisher is an imprint of Macmillan Children's Books, London.
All rights reserved.

Distributed in the U.S. and Canada by Macmillan,
175 Fifth Avenue, New York, NY 10010

Library of Congress Cataloging-in-Publication Data has been applied for.

978-0-7534-7505-8 (HC)
978-0-7534-7492-1 (PB)

Kingfisher books are available for special promotions and premiums. For details contact:
Special Markets Department, Macmillan, 175 Fifth Avenue, New York, NY 10010.

For more information, please visit www.kingfisherbooks.com

Printed in China
9 8 7 6 5 4 3 2 1
1TR/0219/WKT/DIG(MA)/128MA

BACKYARD BOOKS

Are you a Centipede?

Judy Allen and Fiona Osbaldstone

KINGFISHER

LONDON & NEW YORK

Are you a centipede?

If so, what kind are you? Perhaps you are a geophilid centipede. Geophilid means "earth-loving."

If you are, your mother
looks like this . . .

. . . and so does your father.

Your mother laid a lot of
tiny eggs, probably in the
earth or maybe under a
loose bit of tree bark.

She was a good mother. She curled her body around the batch of eggs to keep them safe and warm.

When you hatch you are very small.
Your body is divided into sections, with
a pair of legs on each section.

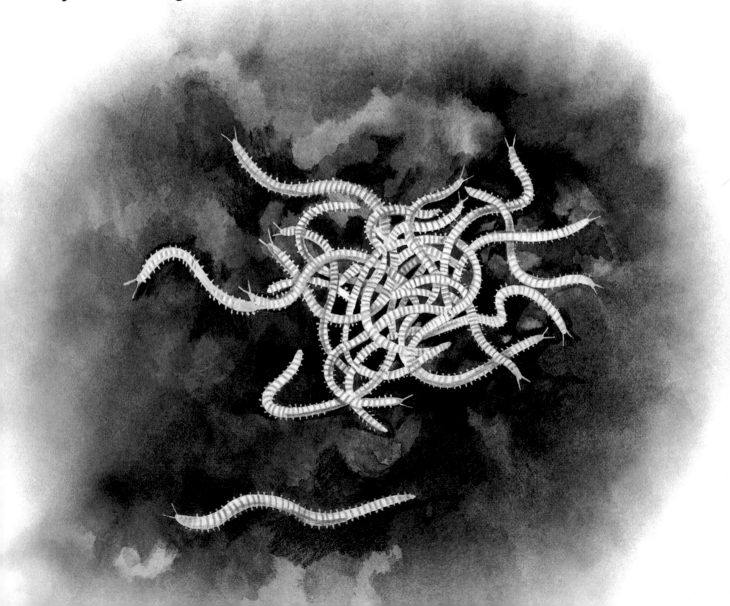

Cent-i-pede means "one hundred feet"—but no centipede ever has exactly one hundred.

You may have more. You probably have fewer.

You have an exoskeleton.

That means your skeleton is outside your body, not inside it like the skeletons of birds or mammals.

You will grow—but your exoskeleton can't grow with you. You will have to break out of it and leave it behind. Climbing out of it is hard work.

You will have a new exoskeleton underneath but it will take a little time to become strong.

You can't see at all well.

Find your way by using your antennae at each end of your body. Live in dark, damp places and go out at night. Avoid daylight if you can.

Luckily you have a flat head and body.
This makes it easy to burrow into soil or
slide under logs, stones, or leaves.

Your body is very flexible. In fact you can tie yourself in a knot. This is handy if you need to sleep in a small space.

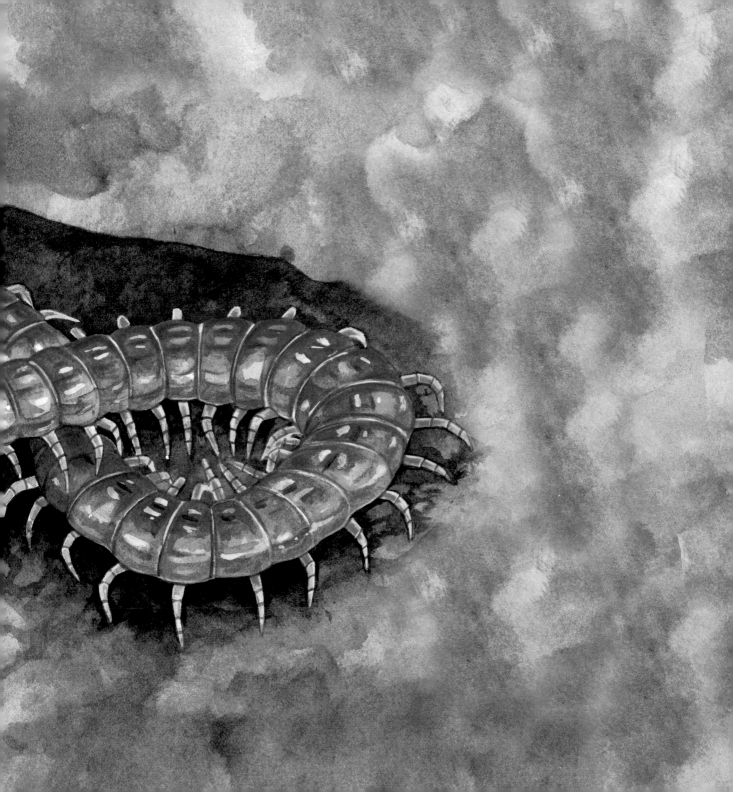

You must eat. Earthworms are nourishing.
Pill bugs are tasty. You will also find all kinds
of tiny creatures that live in the earth.

Your front legs are claws for
catching your food. You have a gland
full of venom just behind each claw.

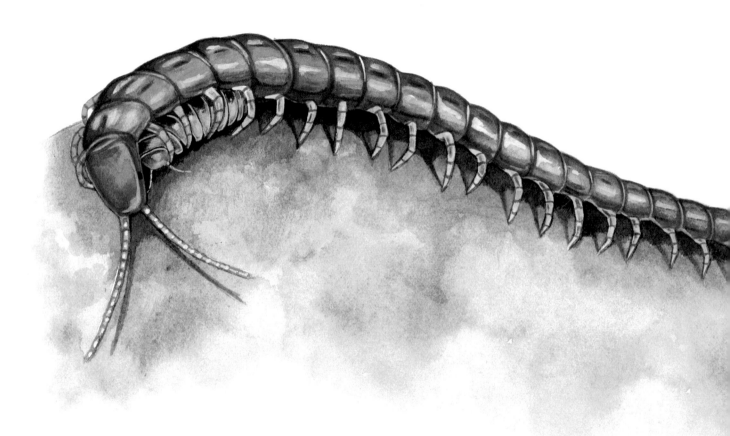

Inject your prey with this
venom and kill it quickly.

Your legs are short but
you can move quite FAST
if you need to.

This is good because
there are dangers out
there, even at night.

Shrews and moles like to eat
you, and so do frogs, toads,
snakes, and birds.

You might even be eaten
by other centipedes!

Here's a useful tip. If an enemy grabs you but only gets hold of some of your legs—leave those legs in its mouth and escape on the ones you have left.

Don't worry, new legs will
gradually grow to fill the gaps.

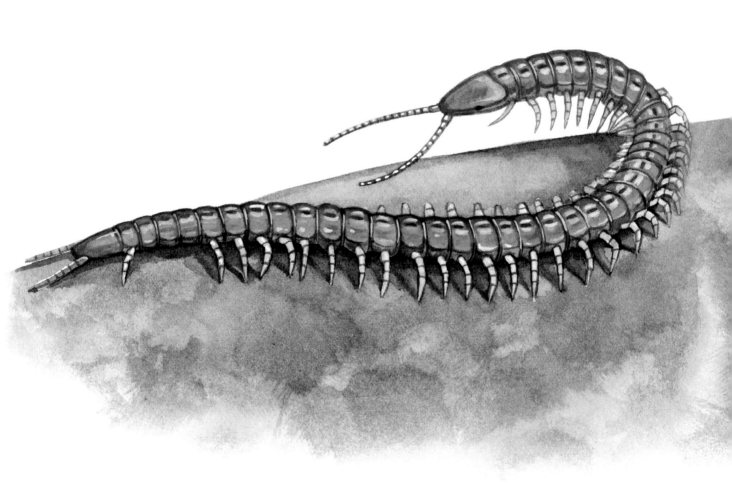

You may meet someone who looks like this. This is a millipede. It has two pairs of legs on each section of its body.

The word milli-pede means "one thousand feet"— but no millipede ever has that many feet.

Millipedes eat leaf litter, which is a mixture of rotted leaves, twigs, bark, and fungus.

The millipede is S-L-O-W but that doesn't matter.

Its food never runs away.

However, if you look a bit like this . . .

or this

or this

you are not a centipede.

You are . . .

...a human child.

You haven't got lots of legs.

Your skeleton is
inside your body,
not outside.

You probably can't tie yourself in a knot.

Never mind, you can do
a great many things a
centipede can't.

Best of all you are never,
ever, ever going to be
eaten by a shrew.

Did You Know...

... centipedes live in all parts of the world except Antarctica.

... there may be up to 8,000 different species of centipede. Only about 3,000 have been named and studied—so far.

... many species of centipede have no eyes at all. Some species have very simple eyes that can only see the difference between dark and light.

... geophilids, like the one in this book, are small and their claws are not strong enough to pierce healthy human skin.

... some tropical centipedes are BIG, as much as 12 inches (30 centimeters) long. Their bite is dangerous to humans.